TOOLS FOR TEACHERS

- **ATOS:** 0.7
- **GRL:** C
- **WORD COUNT:** 32

- **CURRICULUM CONNECTIONS:** community

Skills to Teach

- **HIGH-FREQUENCY WORDS:** a, Dad, get, go, I, makes, Mom, some, the, to
- **CONTENT WORDS:** friend, letter, mail, package, postcard, post office, stamps, visit
- **PUNCTUATION:** periods, apostrophe, exclamation point
- **WORD STUDY:** long /a/, spelled ai (mail); short /e/, spelled e (letter), ie (friend); /j/, spelled ge (package); multisyllable words (letter, office, package, postcard, visit)
- **TEXT TYPE:** descriptive recount

Before Reading Activities

- Read the title and give a simple statement of the main idea.
- Have students "walk" though the book and talk about what they see in the pictures.
- Introduce new vocabulary by having students predict the first letter and locate the word in the text.
- Discuss any unfamiliar concepts that are in the text.

After Reading Activities

Invite children to name friends or family members they would like to greet by letter. Repeat each name, and then ask the children to predict the first letter of each. Write the names on the board, clearly pronouncing each sound as you write. Then as a group compose a letter to be sent to each named person indicating that he or she was in the students' thoughts today. Provide each student with a copy of the letter to be given or mailed to the chosen recipients.

Tadpole Books are published by Jump!, 5357 Penn Avenue South, Minneapolis, MN 55419, www.jumplibrary.com

Copyright ©2018 Jump. International copyright reserved in all countries. No part of this book may be reproduced in any form without written permission from the publisher.

Editorial: Hundred Acre Words, LLC **Designer:** Anna Peterson

Photo Credits: 123RF: Joyce Rector, 6–7. Getty: Andy Crawford, 4–5; Don Hammond, 10–11; Fabio Cardoso, 8–9; Found Image Holdings Inc, 12–13. iStock: oneblink-cj, 14–15; Peloria, cover. Shutterstock: Kara Grubis, 4–5; Ken Wolter, 2–3; Mega Pixel, 1; Prostock-studio, 4–5; Shablon, 12–13.

Library of Congress Cataloging-in-Publication Data
Names: Donner, Erica, author.
Title: Post office / by Erica Donner.
Description: Minneapolis, MN: Jump!, Inc., (2017) | Series: Around town | Includes index.
Identifiers: LCCN 2017041234 (print) | LCCN 2017032115 (ebook) | ISBN 9781624967153 (ebook) | ISBN 9781620319338 (hardcover: alk. paper) | ISBN 9781620319345 (pbk.)
Subjects: LCSH: Postal service—Juvenile literature.
Classification: LCC HE6078 (print) | LCC HE6078 .D66 2017 (ebook) | DDC 383—dc23
LC record available at https://lccn.loc.gov/2017041234

AROUND TOWN

POST OFFICE

by Erica Donner

TABLE OF CONTENTS

tadpole
books

POST OFFICE

Let's go to the post office.

letter

Gabe Kaufman
5357 Marker Street
Brighton, MN 55112

Mom sends a letter.

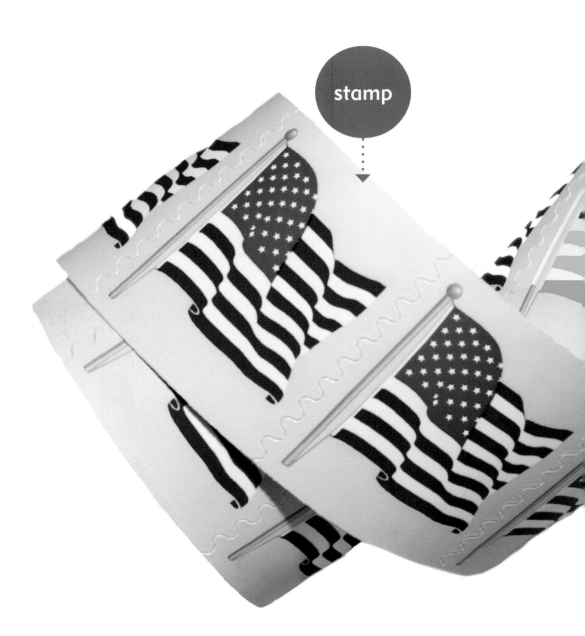

stamp

Gran buys some stamps.

Dad gets his mail.

Spot makes a friend.

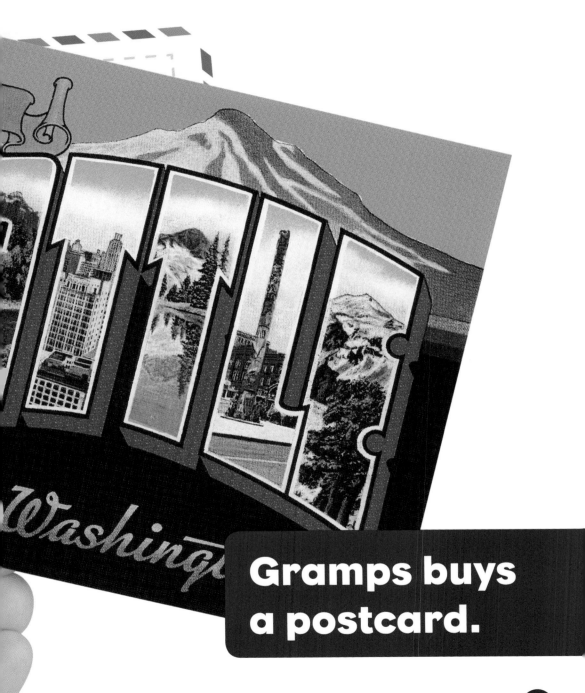

Gramps buys a postcard.

I get a package!

WORDS TO KNOW

letter

mail

package

postcard

post office

stamps

INDEX